ONCE REMOVED

ONCE REMOVED

poems by Nancy Pagh

Chuckanut 2016

Poems for Elizabeth, a true
inspiration, a beautiful
voice, and advocate who
really does change the world
with poetry.

xx,
Nancy Pagh.

MoonPathPress

Poetry

ISBN 978-1-936657-20-9

Cover art by Kathy Hastings:
Patch of Blue, photo encaustic, 8" x 21"

Author photo by Anita K. Boyle, Egress Studio Press

Design by Tonya Namura
using Minion Pro and Avenir Next

MoonPath Press is dedicated to publishing
the finest poets of the U.S. Pacific Northwest

MoonPath Press
PO Box 1808
Kingston, WA 98346

MoonPathPress@yahoo.com

http://MoonPathPress.com

ACKNOWLEDGEMENTS

Lana Hechtman Ayers, Kelli Russell Agodon, and Brenda Miller provided much feedback and support on the completion and arrangement of this manuscript. Mary Cornish, Maria McLeod, and Judy Kleinberg added the stimulating companionship and critique of a writing group. Judy Kleinberg and Luther Allen introduced me to a collaborative writing method I changed into the "textidermy" form. Thank you all!

Many thanks to the editors of these fine publications for first publishing the following poems: *Canadian Literature*, "Tides" and "Cuttings"; *Conversations across Borders*, "Quilts" and "Ceilings"; *Crab Creek Review*, "Cuts" and "Rivers"; *Fire on Her Tongue: An Anthology of Contemporary Women's Poetry*, "Kites"; *Floating Bridge Review*, "That Year"; *Jeopardy*, "Bones" and "Doors"; *Pif Magazine*, "Trails" and "Fingertips"; *Prairie Schooner*, "Trying," "Octopus," and "Before"; *RHINO*, "Tents" and "Eels"; *Valparaiso Poetry Review*, "Oars."

The section titled "After" was first published as a hand-numbered chapbook edition of 400 copies by Floating Bridge Press, Seattle, WA. A special thank you to Kathleen Flenniken and to all the editors at FBP.

"Trails" was illustrated and published as a letterpress broadside by the talented Joe Green at The Peasandcues Press.

Each poem in this collection riffs on and speaks with previously published poetry; these works are acknowledged in the notes.

CONTENTS

v   Acknowledgements

I: **AFTER**
5   After
7   Love Song
10   That Year
12   Octopus
13   A Day Comes
14   You are the Shape
16   I Like to Be Still
17   Before
18   Warnings
19   Whatcom Falls Park Today
20   Safe
22   Relic
24   Trying

II: **FRAUDULENT CREATURES
(A TEXTIDERMY GALLERY)**
29   A Swenson Skvader
31   The Hayden Jackalope
32   A Williams Species of Hodag
33   Gorgon, Plath *var.*
35   Roethke's Fur-Bearing Trout
37   The Brooks Gryphon
38   The Crozier Selkie
39   Clifton's Tartary Lamb
41   Bishop's Shore Muddler
       (*Vitrysk strandmuddlare*)
43   The Carruth Wolpertinger
45   Ono No Komachi's Unicorn
       (Three Small Specimens)
46   The Siren of Millay

III: ONCE REMOVED

49 Highways
50 Tides
51 Cuttings
52 Bones
53 Tents
54 Kites
55 Ferns
56 Pillows
57 Doors
58 Gutters
59 Cuts
60 Eels
61 Channels
62 Oars
63 Quilts
64 Ceilings
65 Stones
66 Rivers
67 Horizons
68 Trees
69 Sleeves
70 Watercolors
71 Barnacles
72 Fingertips
73 Trails

75 Notes

81 About the Author

Once removed: related, but of different generations

ONCE REMOVED

I: AFTER

AFTER

After Emily Dickinson

> *After great pain a formal feeling comes—*
> *The nerves sit ceremonious like tombs;*
> *The stiff Heart questions—was it He that bore?*
> *And yesterday—or centuries before?*

After great pain, a formal feeling comes
buttoning up the naked parts that pressed
themselves against another and so fully

dressed you walk out onto the street
backward for days at a time precisely undoing
everything from the moment a voice first pierced

some cell, some little sleeping room of yourself
that had been so quiet and clean
and all the pictures straight on their walls.

And you imagine you will write sonnets now,
for the rest of your life. Not Gerald Stern's kind,
but ones with meter, rhyme, and fourteen lines

because you were someone capable
of love, and that deserves formal recognition
and the careful arrangement of everything

from now on. Or I'm thinking the sestina
may be your form: six stanzas six lines long,
lines inevitably ending *lead* and *stone* and *snow*

although the ghazal provides opportunity
to show you can sign your own name
in the spelling of *malignancy.*

This is the Hour of Hosiery and Funeral Dress,
remembered—if outlived—in zippered verse
and neatly pressed, unless you let it go—

LOVE SONG

After T. S. Eliot

> *Let us go then, you and I,*
> *When the evening is spread out against the sky*
> *Like a patient etherized upon a table;*
> *Let us go, through certain half-deserted streets,*

Let us go then, you and me,
when the gray clouds rest like scree
poised above the residential lots
and SUVs, the white sedans and minivans
arranged into their stanzas.

Don't ask me why.
Don't ask me why just yet.

And the rain comes.
The rain licks the bumpers and the wiper blades.
The rain rubs itself on oiled pavement and makes
its iridescent sigh, jaywalks on Euclid
toward the A&P, remembers salt
then curls once about the drain hole
and goes to sea.

In apartment complex windows
vague phosphorescent light from TV glows
and infomercial voices that the women disregard
murmur remedies they have no use for;
the small shy cats emerge from furniture
to find the pockets bodies will provide
for them—the shallow bowl of pelvis, soft
seam between half-opened thighs
the fault along one's side
as the arm goes slack.

In the room the men are watching scenes
pornographic on computer screens.

And what if you extend your long
worn self along a length of couch and drop
your gone-gray head into my lap,
unclose your eyes as I
unfix your necktie's simple pin,
draw a blanket, tuck you in;
what if I should dare to touch
the warm bare place you're slightly bald—
a naked pulse of who you are, a current
running corridors toward my sex
(as when my foot soles pressed
against the still-hot metal faucet in a bath)
and I am still, and abluted—
What then?

In the room you're watching **HD** scenes
pornographic on computer screens.

And what if revolution destroyed it
destroyed us all
with obscene gesture, whelming call
toward routine urge and empty pleasure,
apprenticed us to one master
whose only name is Friction.

I know it all already; I know it all.
Know you have chosen lovers
content to play a role—Lolita or a bondage queen
posed upon a straight-back chair;
your cock malingers in her hair

•

8

then slips inside the smile she wears.
You disappear.

．．．．．

The rain comes.
The rain lacks some
essential detachment yet falls
so earnest so uncool upon our bodies
upon our vehicles alike.

I should have been a pair
instead.

．．．．．

The virgins are thirty.
The virgins are thirty and forty and going
to the sperm bank.
The medical technician witnesses
immaculate conception every day,
drives a white sedan, parks carefully,
turns on his home computer.
I have seen him heat his dinner in the microwave.
He knows everybody's getting laid
but him. But how should he presume?

In lab coat Monday afternoons
he stirs, dissolves, with sugar spoons
the Sweet'N Low, the saccharine, and then
imagines online sirens giving head
while women ring the waiting room.
I do not think he'll sing to them.

THAT YEAR

After Sharon Olds

> *The year of the mask of blood, my father*
> *hammering on the glass to get in*
> *was the year they found her body in the hills,*
> *in a shallow grave, naked, white as*

"The truth is, I do indulge myself a little more in pleasure,
knowing that this is the proper age of my life to do it...."
> —*Samuel Pepys*

The year I lost sixty pounds and fell against
better judgment in love with a colleague, dark-eyed
man said *I love women* left a poem on my desk
in a business-size envelope saying he could imagine
my nipples pink as shells scrubbed clean by sand—

That was his year of excuses: a wife lying
beneath her lover's body in Pittsburgh now
while his own flared raw like a nerve each morning
until the first cigarette. The papers to grade, intractable
fleas, the unreasonably gentle-faced moon.

The year he taped a quote by Samuel Pepys to his door,
began sleeping with his student, girl arrested
in a state of teenager tube tops, sparkle make-up,
wax-candy lips mouthing *so hot for Daddy*
and clearly no stranger herself to abuse.

My year of excuses: no one teaches a man how to live
when marriage goes off like a bomb, when sixty terrorizes
the brainpan and the girl seems willing, the porn
circumstantial, the lewd jokes and insults and anger
just part of this picture of human despair, and well—

•

That was the year the spectacle happened
on television, Abu Ghraib prisoners strapped
and hooded, penises wired to electrical currents, soft
sacred hair unwound and bodies positioned like women
taking it while privates posed and others shot

their pictures as mementos, and still I did not see
beyond my own one bruise, my own imagined loss
until the day I googled my colleague's name
and found his poem about gagging this girl, tying her
down, admiring the wrists he had welted and burned

and that was the end of the year of detainment,
the end of excuses, the first-mute sensation of traveling out
to reach the understanding that this is all
connected, this broad insidious leash disguised
as duty, or love, or a little more pleasure.

OCTOPUS

After Pat Lowther

> *The octopus is beautifully*
> *functional as an umbrella;*
> *at rest a bag of rucked skin*
> *sags like an empty scrotum*

Some men are beautifully
dysfunctional when you first
know them; the loss
of youth, integrity, or wife clear
in each lovely unsure gesture
you mistake for tenderness

but taking flight from you: look
how sure and purposeful
in every part:
their smooth machinery
moving efficiently away
as if engineered by Leonardo
or a god who gave the octopus,
not you, its obscuring spurt
and perfect whirl of gears,
its three hearts   running

A DAY COMES

After C. P. Cavafy

> *A day comes to some people when*
> *they must pronounce the great Yes or the great No.*
> *It is instantly clear who has the Yes within, ready;*

A day comes to some people when
we are taken about the throat and pushed
to hardwood floor; knees pin us, a rough
hand cups the side of the face before
slamming the head again, again to oak.

And we are asked to pronounce the great
Yes, or the great No. As if it was not clear
enough already, that Yes brought us here,
keeps us still. Yes, we thought, Yes:
a floor would give.

YOU ARE THE SHAPE

After Olena Kalytiak Davis

> *the fields and fields*
> *of lowly lupine*
> *have already slipped*
> *your mind*

the ridges of sand
the furrows, rib bones of sand
the outer coast of your mind
slipping away

returns with a glass circle, a japanese float
a swirl of kelp
some medical waste you kick along high-tide's mark

from a distance
that kelp is an animal all made of tails

keep walking

the field guide to the littoral zone is on a shelf in your room
the latin name for green anemone hardly concerns
only the pendulous breasts stretching from stone
the shallow pool's surface an oval below:
the sculpin, the miniature crabs contained in contour and
     fold

breast bone of sand breaks underfoot
what does it matter
that you are the shape of a body he once
had opportunity to love but turned down

•

and why did you do that? imagining he could imagine you
as you are, never seen, chartbook drawn
with fingernail tongue soul
unwritten still

periwinkles write it slow

he had already figured out
what was important to him, hadn't he?
said he was a ship going down, radio out, wind
lots of it and no hope
closing the watertight doors

and did you ask for this?

surely you had
to walk so far from what is kind and good
to know it

there's beach glass now, sugared, dull

brain coiled in a shell

can anyone hold the shape of anything?

I LIKE TO BE STILL

After Pablo Neruda

> *I like for you to be still: it is as though you were absent,*
> *and you hear me from far away and my voice does not touch you.*
> *It seems as though your eyes had flown away*
> *and it seems that a kiss had sealed your mouth.*

I like to be still: it is as though there never was
such a thing as waking, and crows beyond the window
are distant as beaches with private hotels.
No one strips the bedding. No one sweeps the sand.

Everyone chooses not to touch some things.
And the soul of these things goes on dreaming
and seems far away like our own red birth.
I am like the word *annunciation*.

I like to be still in this room in the morning.
A sleeping cat pushes his back to my spine.
There is nothing to look forward to
so much as fondling his head and the sound he will make.

You misunderstand my silence. All things are my soul
and the quietest things are me most of all. This is true:
I am not entertaining in the way that you want.
My breasts never warranted an exclamation mark.

I like to be still: it is as though there never was
possibility then possibility taken away beyond windows
and stars and the high afternoon so remote like you
and everyone choosing to touch other things.

BEFORE

After Chris Forhan

> *The moon and constellations were not then.*
> *Nor tides, horizons, graves—all was ocean,*
> *and we lived on the great whale's back*
> *a whale so vast in none of our roaming*

The letter and inks were not then.
Nor binding, period, spaces between—all was oyster shell
and butter clam. The raven's *groak*. The muskrat's little hand,
a pattern pressed in crust of sand
was delible. No metaphor at all. We lived
each in our own body and happy there.
Let me tell you how clean the rain it ran.
Let me tell you: you were among us.
Do you understand I speak of desire? About the sky
I say nothing at all. Only the birds dreamed their falling.
There was the practice of cupping things and
someone touched your cheek. You were likened
to no object whatsoever. That was our practice, also.
Then somebody said beautiful. Somebody wrote a poem.
And somebody wasn't, and hurt.
I know fire was involved: we built the flame and made the
      char
that wrote it.

WARNINGS

After Claudia Emerson

> *There were warnings: he had, at forty, never*
> *married; he was too close to his mother,*
> *calling her by her given name, Manuela,*
> *ah, Manuela—like a lover; even her face*

There were warnings: when he left his wife he took
only a television to watch forensic crime-scene dramas.
Pixelated putrefactions flickered in his living room but
he'd have told you he jerked off to the red-head investigator.

He drove a Honda Civic with five o'clock shadow
moldered on its pallid paint, the interior a graveyard
for carcasses of ancient Happy Meal figurines. At fifty-six,
his children had grown past him. He never failed to order

eternal life from a waitress or ask *Would you mind*
if I know your age? He said what he'd do to me
with his penis and sighed, then added *I guess you'd want*
more. He kept photos of himself naked in a bedside drawer.

So we were not lovers. But it ended badly
because I loved him and had not been loved before.

I was old enough to be someone's grandma, aware I would fall
in my own dry grave without knowing a man's body except
my father's, as I'd held the urinal for him when he died. I saw
that a man's piss is thick and dark. I learned where to leave it.

WHATCOM FALLS PARK TODAY

After Peter Pereira

Today when I looked in the mirror
I saw my father looking back.
I like walking alone at night.
One can be happy not only without love,

Today when I looked in the road
I saw the gray squirrel's viscera
trail from its body and thought
is that why we call them entrails.
I like walking alone in the park.
One can be happy in cotton shorts
even though synthetic dries faster.
Dogs do not understand personal boundaries.
There are such things as red dragonflies;
I saw five rest on this iron bridge last summer.
What can you do about a creosote stain?
Rabbit! no rabbit: white grocery sack
handles tied up as ears. What's with
the used doggie poop bags, twisted
and set on the trail like wrong dim sum?
I have always found that garter snakes
remind me of zippers, but not known why.
I would have cared more
if it had been a native red squirrel.
I know what that says about me.
That's a thrush. It sounds
how I felt to fingerpaint when I was six.
Now I am glad I chose the caffeinated tea.
Waterfall~waterfall~waterfall~stream.
Haruspicy is the word I almost thought.
I will cook the rice in chicken stock.
I am thinking: will I cut the yellow squash
in rounds or cubes and
not of you, sorry man. Not you.

SAFE

After Susan Mitchell

> *He said I want to kiss you in a way*
> *no one has ever kissed you before, a kiss*
> *so special you will never forget and no one will ever*

I tell myself it's time   it's time
to try again the early morning small birds half asleep
cotton sheeting dry and sweet   no cause to think of him
flexing tip of finger go   begin

the boy from college years   and years
adored a little stutter his, an affectation, winsome
lose some   he stood on deck between me and the sun
I swear to god Apollo. I swear to God

we drank some beer. Imagine had we moved
into the cabin   and drifting on had sacrificed
the view of Mount Rainier. Think that little scar
his cocker spaniel drew. Think perfect pitch of blue

how kisses knew to land on him   his throat
blushed sometimes   yes time imagine
tag of ear on tongue   and how much once
I loved his square-tipped fingers fondling

sheets, which means ropes if you know anything
about sailing. He was tentative and I
was ugly and smart.   There is nothing feasible
about a scene where he touches me   like that

time I was hanging with the janitor in city hall
we lay on the carpet and kissed by the vacuum
I pulled his Pine-sol grip to my chest and
he packed up his solvents and left.   That's all

•

20

except the cousin who tied me with a cord
blacked my eye   showed me his cock   asked
could he put it in and pee? Chick-a-dee-dee-dee.
No. Dee dee dee. And he didn't. No biggie.

Make something up now   please stranger hurry
along or it's him who was cruel and crude
his mid-life crisis   his missing tooth   his greasy sneer
and fear. Him joke and never feel. Him disappear.

Little girl I   wanted nothing   more
than sleep all alone in a tent on the shore   while
parents afloat on the bay. Thirteen
they promised   then thought better: our girl

in the ferns like an egg. Imagine their anxiety
unzips a nylon shell   someone's hands on skin
of a daughter   flutter owl, flutter   who?
the black gelid sea stretched flat as a membrane.

Sometimes in the years that followed
I wished my parents had understood the truth
and told it to me straight: *Do everything you want.*
My god, you are completely safe.

RELIC

After Ellen Bass

What if you knew you'd be the last
to touch someone?
If you were taking tickets, for example,

What if we knew I'd be the last
woman to fall in love
with someone
bad?

If women from now on
were to catapult themselves
into loving
someone different
someone lacking the smoker's cough
I hear from his side of the bookstore
interrupting the poet
like he always does

then what a wonderful relic
my point of view would be,
enjoyed & honored for anachronistic rarity
with neat and accurate labels
for the way it used to see
his sagging bellyfat
as something marvelous and sweet
beyond all measure
and brown folds of his triple chins
dear to me as rhyme and meter.

I suppose some would pay to see his perversion
draped across the pedestal I'd held,
its fuzz arranged in seeming soft
ironic lines and

•

22

in a small glass box, the word I made
for the color of his eyes.

TRYING

After Marge Piercy

> *The people I love the best*
> *jump into work head first*
> *without dallying in the shallows*
> *and swim off with sure strokes almost out of sight.*

The people I love best are the ones who try: the aged who rise
early each damp morning and part the clump of coffee filters
with arthritic fingers—and the others who stay up
late after working all day in retail, hot pink curl of ear
pressing the receiver, listening to the friend who is selfish
but in agony now. I love the men who are fathers
to children, not buddies not video-game rivals not boys
themselves but clumsy men who ache over the fragility of sons,
but preserve the fragility of sons despite what everyone says.
I love those who feel no skill has come to them innate,
who will hold their small inland dogs again and again
above the sea on vacation, to watch in amazement
the knowing animal body that paddles through air. I love
the B+ student. The thick-chinned girl always picked
fourth when choosing sides for the softball team.
The lover who says it first. The lover who says it second
after a long, long pause. The lover who says it knowing
the answer is no, no, I am too broken. People who knit
things together. People willing to take things apart
and roll all the strands of yarn into new balls for next time.
The woman who loaded her backseat full of blankets and
    drove
for three days to the hurricane site. Even the loafer who tries
his mother's patience, who quietly speculates and eventually
decodes the universe for us all. Believe me, I have tried
to love others, the meager personalities who charm and
    butter,

•

the jaded the cynics the players and floaters all safe
in their cages, this life no responsibility they can own.
They see it too—how trying is always a risk,
a kind of vulnerability some choose for ourselves because
our fathers taught us well, our fathers taught us to try
to remain as fragile and full as this world that loves us.

II: FRAUDULENT CREATURES
(*A TEXTIDERMY GALLERY*)

A SWENSON SKVADER

The summer that I was ten—
can it be there was only one
summer when I was ten? It must

have been a long one then—
I imagined I'd live on an island
in a cabin of weather-bleached planks

beside a stand of broad-leaf maples.
I wouldn't have a job in the cannery
or picking strawberries on my knees.

The tide would boil in the channel—
I could hear it at night
from my bedroom—thrumming

slick fronds of the kelp's amber hair.
I would dig butter clams all morning
and eat them in the afternoon.

At the end of day, someone
might pull a boat to safety at my dock
and keep company. But on an island

I could always see that coming.
Now I am fifty, in a house on a rock.
A channel of traffic cuts close

to the porch; it snorts
and it wallows and passes nearby.
It is perfectly clear how

we make our lives islands,
carefully removing the dock for winter
or losing it anyway in a freak summer storm.

But still some nights, at eleven
or ten, my poems become planks;
the fruit of the maples—

samaras, propellers—words drifting
to land. Yours is the boat,
the moon shines its gunwale;
yours is the choice in the channel.

THE HAYDEN JACKALOPE

Some days my father got up early,
put his clothes on in the blueback cold.
With cracked hands that ached
from labor in the mill, he made
the banked fire blaze from pieces
of wood that had washed up on beaches.
He carried them carefully home
through the summers, carefully split
them alone with his hatchet:
I remember those fires in winter,
the smell of the cedar, perfume of the pitch,
damp sputter of alder coaxed by the kindling
and being naked with my sister
after bathing, naked and wet
in front of a fire, unacquainted with shame,
then the cold hall to white sheets and sleep.
I don't know about your father. But
if you lived in the twentieth century
I imagine you never thanked him, either,
not really. The beaches men walked
and the drift they could find then
were private and burned
through that silence.

A WILLIAMS SPECIES OF HODAG

When I am alone I am happy.
The air is cool. The sky is
flecked and splashed and wound
with color. When I reach
the shore trail I notice
eight pairs of seals in the bay,
dark wet heads bulbous
and nodding together.
The current moves across
their backs and slight
upwellings shadow their turns.
Last year's pups are heavy
as their mothers now or
perhaps pairs are reuniting.

Are not my friends as dear to me
as maple leaves across the trail
unstitching themselves
from stem and form?
Look. There are no seals,
but sixteen bull kelp in the bay.
Held fast to a common reef
each bulb is separate as my head,
ripe floats in coiling tide.
Friend, it seems to me the
seals do not want it otherwise.

GORGON, PLATH *VAR.*

He must have died young, driving
his father's tractor along the culvert,
along sweet timothy grass and distracted
by the graceful implacability of that hawk
as the little birds chased and raged headlong.
Or from ice on the rigging, coating and coating
the cables and crab cages, laying heavier
through a black Bering night, cold enough
to freeze salt water blown through the air,
until the boat staggered and dropped him,
just a high-school kid, into silence.
He might have been drinking one night.
That would do it. Or the city machines
caught into his finger and pulled
him to violence, addiction, a ripping
despair, a fall from some high building.

One of my girlfriends believes the right man
is born for each of us, is waiting
for the appropriate moment to arrive in our lives.
I think mine died young. He is learning
peacefulness now, lying by himself quietly
as light lies on a white wall, on hands,
and he is doing things with his hands
to my tea set. I am a nun now, I have never
been so pure. To lie turned up and utterly empty,
how free it is, you have no idea how free—
the peacefulness is so big it dazes you.
I see myself, fat, ridiculous, an awful baby
without a face, wanting to efface myself:
I have let her slip. I shut my mouth
on him like a communion wafer. Now
out of sheer love of me, each day's light slowly widens
and slowly thins. He stays in his country.

•

His emissaries pass the way gulls pass inland
or they stay for a while like unexpected tulips
pressing up from sweet timothy.

ROETHKE'S FUR-BEARING TROUT

I thought the west wind called me from my bed.
I woke to sleep, and took my waking slow
the night the river ran so hard. I followed,
felt my fate in what I cannot fear.

I woke to sleep, and took my waking slow
across the moonlit lawns, across the road.
I felt my fate in what I cannot fear.
I climbed the fallen cedars, moved beyond.

Across the moonlit lawns, across the road,
I learned by going where I had to go.
I climbed the fallen cedars, moved beyond
what falls away, is always, and is near.

I learned by going where I had to go.
I followed to the river bed and plunged:
what fell away, is always, and is near
swirled behind my knees and tried to run.

I followed through the river bed and plunged:
I heard my being dance from ear to ear.
Trout swirled behind my knees and tried to run:
of those so close beside me, which were you?

I heard my being dance from ear to ear.
I clenched the underwater moss, was lost.
Of those so close beside me, which were you?
Until the wind stopped, I knew why I came.

I clenched the underwater moss, was lost
to you and me; I swayed outside myself.
When hard wind stops, we forget why it came.
Wind takes the tree; but who can tell us how?

To you and me, I swayed outside myself.
To other ways of knowing, I swayed in.
Wind takes the tree; but I can tell you how
the fallen cedar keeps the forest steady.

To other ways of knowing, I sway in
and out: I wake to sleep. I feel to think.
I shake the tender parts that would lie steady.
I listen when the wind calls me from bed.

THE BROOKS GRYPHON

In little jars and cabinets of my will
I let myself believe that love was good.
I held my honey and I stored my bread.

A grizzly shook his head from side to side.
He ambled slowly, sniffed the stuff inside
my little jars, the cabinets of my will.

He wasn't hungry, but was incomplete.
He pushed his trail until the alder gave;
I gave my honey and I gave my bread.

I hoped that, when the devil days of hurt
resumed, when rain returned I'd catch it in
my empty jars and cabinets of my will.

I'd drink. Become the rain I loved and fall
as rain falls, on its knees. But darkness stopped
the bear that licked my honey, tore my bread.

No man has given any word but Wait.
But now my dreams, my works leap out instead
from little jars and cabinets of my will.
I eat this honey, smear it on my bread.

THE CROZIER SELKIE

Sometimes my body leaves me, goes into
another room and locks the door. There
alone it finds what it was looking for.

The insect on a wall, the paper map
of counties iridescent in each wing:
sometimes a body finds me, goes into

me as a fishing line that falls through layers
more compressed each than the one before.
A leaded hook finds what it's fishing for.

The spark of fresh-laid asphalt, crows and glints
from trailer parks, magenta rhododendrons—
my body seems to leaf, to incandesce

sometimes, becoming what it sees and knows.
The little arm and neck hairs register
alone it found what it was it looking for.

I sit without a book or anything
resembling love, yet loving how sometimes
my body leaves me, goes into the world
alone and finds what we are looking for.

CLIFTON'S TARTARY LAMB

well, girl, goodbye:
after thirty-eight years,
thirty-eight years you
shifted subtly one day
redistributed without quake
without ash just
repositioned yourself down
stream, carried below the
bones and ridges
lower down, underneath
the places you had sat atop
before.

you fell one summer
afternoon as i walked to the mailbox
in shorts and observed
my thighs now had a rhythm
all their own a
sort of seismic back beat
to my purposeful stride
and gelatinous, too.

my fat, you fell along the gravel
driveway causing
me to look in the mirror
upon returning to the house
and make the abrupt
acquaintance of each new jowl,
the flap beneath each arm.

it seemed as if you continued
falling over the edge of my bed
as i sat there and dressed

•

each morning
all that long week.

now it is done,
the erosion of former full
peaks of breasts i so fervently
hid under sweatshirts.

goodbye solid ledge of belly,
supple timbers my forearms
were, broad landscape
that had been my own face.

you made me
sentimental and notice
for the first time ever
i had been so beautiful
in the first place.

BISHOP'S SHORE MUDDLER
(*VITRYSK STRANDMUDDLARE*)

I caught my tremendous father
and held him beside the hospital bed
half out of the sheets, with the IV
fast in the corner of his arm.
He didn't fight.
He hadn't fought at all.
He hung a grunting weight,
battered and venerable
and homely. Here and there
his pale skin hung like crepe,
like ancient wallpaper:
its pattern of veins and moles
and sunburn stain made
shapes like full-blown anemone
faded and lost
through age.
He was speckled with tags and barnacles,
infested with flakes from his scalp.
While his lungs were breathing in
the terrible oxygen
I looked into his eyes
which were glass frosted somehow
but reminded me now
of the thin layer of indigo
painted beneath the herring's armor;
of crusted circles, puckering stars:
fish scales dried to my body;
how candlefish, swimming,
taper; and why
all rays of light radiate from my head
as I look down into water.
All of it was equally

beautiful then.
When my father clubbed the rock cod
after its furious climb to sunlight
I grew up
to despise violence
but yearning for simple beauty
to haul me up
and overpower me
and in this way
fathers never let us go.

THE CARRUTH WOLPERTINGER

There were so many poems about the deaths of animals.
Wilbur's toad, Kinnell's porcupine, Eberhart's squirrel,
and that poem by someone—Hecht? Merrill?—
about cremating a woodchuck. But mostly
I remember the outrageous number of them,
as if every poet, I too, had written at least
one animal elegy; with the result that once
when I came to a good enough poem by Edwin Brock
about finding a dead fox at the edge of the sea
I could not respond; as if permanent shock
had deadened me. And then after a moment
I began to give way to sorrow (watching myself
sorrowlessly the while), not merely because
part of my being had been violated and annulled,
but because all these many poems over the years
have been necessary—suitable and correct.

Tonight the red-tail hawks line Highway 20.
Posturing their James Dean shoulders they clench
the human casualty markers. This road
goes to my parents' house (their hawthorn bush,
the honey bees we kept in jam and pickle jars)
and farther back to grandfather's farmhouse, a bright
line of nuisance skunks and foxes strung from the walnut.
Tonight I'm driving with a summer sunset in my eye,
each landmark a memory of some other trip.
Just here, the spot we hit a marten. This shoulder
where we all got out to look at a porcupine's quills.
Mile after mile the crosses appear; I don't know why
we bear more remembrance than the jagged-faced opossum
whose body broke beneath a tire. These crosses
try to mark our difference from the forms that fall
and shatter and serve as their own headstones
until the hawk finds some better purpose.

•

This is the time of finishing off the animals.
They are going away—their fur and wild eyes,
their voices. And this is the time of finishing off
the poems that loved the animals, and the poems that loved
the body, the imagery, the places our animal
selves inhabited, knew. I lived with them fifty years,
poems with skin, with song, with oil-can shacks
and blue Chinese gardens. Eyelash, nautilus,
plump hazelnut shells, the oily fabulation of mackerel—
Spring arriving capitalized, as if delight
were the most serious thing and the world mud-
luscious. Now they are going, almost gone, the old poems
a run of jacks in a dammed creek; their voices
the burrow-nest of a mouse, a softness plowed under
what was the grass.

ONO NO KOMACHI'S UNICORN
(THREE SMALL SPECIMENS)

i

The sponge of moss,
The religion I discarded:
While I contemplate one
My body remembers
The urge to kneel.

ii

Doesn't he realize
I am not like the deer
Shifting the weight of its rack?
I have chosen a wasted life,
A head full of light.

iii

So present am I
My body is a floating weed
Attached at the root.
Were sinking to entice me,
Same root, same depth.

THE SIREN OF MILLAY

No matter what I say
all that I really love
is the rain that flattens on the bay
and the eel-grass in the cove,

the jingle-shells that lie on the beach
at the tide-line, and the trace
of higher tides along the beach beneath
a leaning line of madrona.

After I die, take me to a madrona:
choose one red-boled, round-hipped
and open at the shoulders,
then tie me supine toward the sky

among rubbery leaves or dry ones
(I don't want to fall in the first wind).
Curling red bark of madrona
pulls back from the limbs each summer

and I'll peel too, unwinding from bone.
The quietest places
will come unstitched, until
even the secrets I kept in my belly

sound raucous in the mouths of crows.
The tide will roll an oiled feather, a periwinkle
and me in its long, soft tongue
no matter what it says.

III: ONCE REMOVED

HIGHWAYS

I knew a lot of things

about naming. Chokecherry. Killdeer. Stream violet.

How sailors seek wind and unnamed blue things.

How lightning made fireweed ride its stem,

highways of brightness through open places.

Sleepwalkers tread paths through remembered rooms.

Hands chart upholstered furniture

of former apartments. Landscapes

freighted away. Silt in any stream.

TIDES

Someone plants eel-grass September mornings.

I do the dead-man's float in memory foam.

Fog congeals, grays. Once I rowed a dinghy

against tide I could not out-muscle. Had to land,

wade, pull the boat by its painter. The line

I live on stops at :18 and :46 weekdays.

Some afternoons a bleached moon rises.

Ten thousand vehicles flow past my house.

Moon, no moon, I chart the hours by their whine.

There's a trick with a spoon and some water.

Do it until the mind goes slack.

CUTTINGS

The nice thing about having fins is how

they cut things, serrate the cellophane

of surface tension. I suppose

wings can do this too. Meanwhile

the spine's a stick that pins you straight to the world.

One year I planted rhododendrons in the shade.

Called each one "you," and "you," and "you."

Reasons for being in a garden:

very different from a beach.

Baked shale. Effluvial ooze. Near water green,

far water silver. Black fins cutting the distance.

BONES

The chiropractor's hand finds the bone he desires.

There must be ways to feel, to move. Understory.

Devil's club. Imaginary line from A to B.

Deer watch you attempt the route. They take

the whole garden through delicate faces, removed

from your crash in the sofa. Moments run off.

Hands you knew without holding.

Beds of fingernails. Moons that rose in them.

A boy you memorized. The bones

of an animal you thought you could be.

Black tail. White tail. Gone.

TENTS

It had to do with the moon that night

climbing the boned skirt of a cedar.

Cod respond to a jig's glint just off the reef.

A pan of browning butter above fire. Depths

of various densities and the way light

strikes metal. I remember nothing we spoke,

only smooth whorls of sun-warmed sandstone.

Hairs white on my forearms. A tent

is a small envelope of breath in the forest. A body

wears boy clothes or girl clothes. A chair

straight backed and wooden

is meant to be hung on a wall.

KITES

Some days all I think about is pancakes.

Heavy syrup. Carboholic.

I brush my hair, stroke my teeth with a tongue

like the smallest birds hitting windows.

I knew a horse in Albuquerque. Her rump.

Some kites fly without tails, some

like mice before the tractor's big rubber wheel.

FERNS

Building their pyramids their slivers slower

than sitting on porches peeling the paint

than watching a cabbage moth

make lace of the garden. You can draw

lines and tell anything to get in there.

Once removed from sentiment, the mind's

small fist unfurls one quarter turn per day—

still a kind of crashing through understory, away

from the moment and everyone hiding

in there.

PILLOWS

I think about the morning I meant to kill you.

Driving down the long hill. A pillow in my head.

The kind of summer day you would have liked.

Magnitude of chlorophyll. Immensity of sky.

Now an art gallery featuring nothing but ravens.

One kind of rain smells of copper.

Another kind of rain lets you go.

What about this life is not a place holder?

Some alternate morning I will park in a driveway,

fly through a door. When they say you are dead

a screen having nothing to do with it.

DOORS

The mind sits in its vinyl booth. Wormwood walls

of restaurants from a certain era. A beach. A menu.

Buoys or gulls. Inboard or outboard. A glass

float caught in netting near the register.

Small rooms travel when their doors slide shut.

Push a button. Call yourself back.

Lose it, or don't lose it, in the elevator.

Pop up. Wood float on slack line.

A porpoise drives the distance.

Bottle nose breaking doors in the sea.

GUTTERS

Come over here, it says. A kind of disarrangement

happens. The way fingers explore a plugged gutter.

Or angioplasty a jugular. Finding

damp nests for nothing but moss. Farther

up river than I have ever been, salmon gleam

their union suits. Skeins unwind,

undulate in current. Clot the gravel spawning bed.

A house can smell of stew and domesticity.

The unseen pad flows beneath carpet,

a slate-gray stream the cat divines.

Manages to pee in.

CUTS

A platonic relationship with the world
wears you out, that's for sure. How
close it lets you, never going
all the way. See how the bats cut
darkness with something darker?
The doe rejects a strange fawn.
She snorts in the driveway. There's this
unbearable noise of things passing close.
Things you can lose
without having.

EELS

A cousin, once removed, said the day's sorrow

knew exactly what he needed.

In these moments we call ourselves related.

Grandma born to slide a knife along an eel

in ways only water understands.

I am unclear about the Old Country.

Paintings are places we might have lived,

potatoes we might have salted and eaten.

CHANNELS

The open field. The slow undulation of grass.

A coasting mind blows infinite channels.

Still, this shroud of skin hangs on the face.

A canvas sail sighted long before the ship itself.

Throw a pot at the ocean. Interrupt

the underwater highway a Dungeness travels.

The sea floor is a palimpsest he writes

in oxblood script. Hide a word

for skin, for vanishing in eel grass.

OARS

A father dies in a living room, years ago, in June.

Kicking into action mode, that's one

response to crisis. Or watch movies.

Rock Hudson kissing a woman's neck

and the question of beauty, the Real Self.

Hands on wooden oars. A quiet bay.

Notes each blade drips at the end of a stroke.

Water meeting water. I was a wounded man

in all my girlhood fantasies. Carried, bandaged,

touched. Another self in chambray shirts.

Hospital sheets. A father knows you.

Death takes who he knows away.

In a life beneath this life I am Rock Hudson.

I am also the neck and the wind

blowing curtains behind two perfect bodies.

One bends another the way

an oar appears bent from the exact place

it enters water.

QUILTS

Don't tell me morning is not on trial.

How it snuck around the yard. How it cut

the day's page with hands

curled now at my throat. Little

neck animals. Bed's shadow puppets.

The joint in a thumb forecasts change.

Accomplice in the act of getting over

it. No prints. No trace of the struggle.

This room. This light. This quilt

for turning back again and again and again.

CEILINGS

The trivial float off to some other dock

built of gypsum and paint. A ceiling

sees what it sees. Knows what it knows. Lets

down its ropes of oyster seed

to sway in the night. When my mother's hands

left my father, she buried them in a garden.

I don't know the world itself, only a passing

likeness. It calcifies above my bed.

The shells could be ground and mixed into landscapes

disturbed here and there

by hands, by animals taking their rest.

STONES

Breath escaping underwater

runs to meet its mother, sky.

October hair all up in curlers. Because

children protect themselves with names

I say I was a glass jar of mussel shells.

One girl was Billy the Kid. I could be

her horse, she said. As if I was just another person.

A good childhood is hard

to live up to, grow out of. One summer

my girlfriend said I was possessed by the Beatles.

She prayed for me. I floated

on my parents' waterbed, imagining my own death

which I realized is life before childhood.

I was a black stone, its equator

drawn in white to mark

each falling revolution.

RIVERS

Through the park down the road,

a mute river flows without song.

Water scooters resist each embankment.

Skate over trout, the trout

still as stone. I'm home making chili.

Yellow pears line the windowsill.

Their skin hieroglyphics tell nothing but rot.

I am aware the wire beneath that bird

used to transmit *love you, love you, love you*

before this age. But the freezer I know

still hums to the car. I'm in the kitchen

now, listening for something.

Cheek to the dishwasher's breast.

HORIZONS

Sense of humor on the water front. *Horizon Lines*

painted on the side of that ship always docked

here. Something travels though, threading the islands

into the Straight. Perceives a dark blue edge

right out of Georgia O'Keefe, if she had fled the desert, come

to apprehend the wind's relationship with water

and light. Quiet nights, something not regret

runs loose in the brain, a child's tangled crayon line.

Given time, the hand learns to draw

a brown horizon. Perch mill above it.

Technicolor starfish twirl below. Something

not regret signs its name in a corner.

TREES

Fir remain unaware of rugosity, wild roses at their feet.

Wild roses think all day about pink. *Pink, pink, pink.*

The half-life of a poem is the last time you read it.

I drive a purple car, sometimes fast, sometimes too slow.

The look some people can put on their faces.

Ways of measuring and balance often elude me

when I'm not reading. Walking toward the sea

that afternoon, spaces between trees

shining and how the line of thought refracts as

carsgobycarsgobycarsgoby.

SLEEVES

The day wears its long sleeves, wet at the wrists

from tide pools. In the low tide of night

I saw my father clear, heard his tuneless whistle.

Bears turn in kinnikinnick, I suppose. Dreaming

their sockeye, their caves. Not the words *I must remember*

this sound when he's gone. The present situation.

Its tea kettle, tea. The weeding ahead.

The readable gesture of Oregon grape

catching a sleeve to send you away.

WATERCOLORS

Another moment frames another version of the self

for the refrigerator door

then follows the curb down the road.

Rings around each pupil fade,

spread as watercolor meets a page.

Admire the quiet ways a body will collapse.

Feel the earth move as you push off each step.

What mattered in those days?

Other houses, yellow rooms, light touching

an eagle's nest in the forest, space around it

made from the swath cut for a pipeline.

Certain fabrics rustle when you stride.

The desire for companionable sounds.

Who hangs back. Who holds on.

How to angle an ox-hair brush.

BARNACLES

The barnacle builds from rock.

White house, white siding, chimney

streaming feathers red as streaks

through adolescent hair. My friend,

with a knife god ended silence,

invented lips, then wiped his blade.

On one beach a raven settles,

cocks her head to observe

some currency from a country never visited.

How like pockets, the lungs, which a hand never enters.

One thing settles. Another will rise.

Barefoot, feeling the garden for stones,

I notice how soil takes the edge off.

Kneel. Hands flagella,

combing out the hard

parts remaining.

FINGERTIPS

The locust references its leaves through shoji screen.

Along slick banks of morning mind

the obsession with dying. The dead, I think.

A dream I leave dripping, sunlight in my hair.

Yesterday I left a city. Its subways

moved like mice through snakes.

One season pulls away a little, which makes us ache.

I could learn to catch its fingertips.

Look the dark lake in its eye. Touch the wild

yellow iris caught in its lashes.

TRAILS

Old furniture made from sea grasses bent, shellacked.

Yellow Point. Early tea. How morning wipes stars from a
    table,

slides us a plate with an egg. Upcoast

bears turn boulders on beaches, decipher and eat

the tide's arrangements. Stillness is a word

for continuing to exist. For sea lettuce waving

its tarpaulin over a crab. The ability

to carry our freight of flesh

down one trail or another.

NOTES

The "After" section was composed as a series of riffs. Here is an alphabetical bibliography of the specific poems my works are "after":

Ellen Bass, "If You Knew." *The Human Line*. Port Townsend, WA: Copper Canyon Press, 2007.

C. P. Cavafy, "Che Fece...Il Gran Rifiuto." Translated by Aliki Barnstone and Willis Barnstone. *The Collected Poems of C. P. Cavafy*. New York: W. W. Norton & Company, 2006.

Olena Kalytiak Davis, "Saxifrage and Cinquefoil." *And Her Soul Out of Nothing*. Madison: The University of Wisconsin Press, 1997.

Emily Dickinson, F372 ("After great pain, a formal feeling comes—"). *The Poems of Emily Dickinson*, edited by Ralph W. Franklin. Cambridge, MA: Harvard University Press, 1988.

T. S. Eliot, "The Love Song of J. Alfred Prufrock." *T. S. Eliot: Selected Poems*. San Diego: Harcourt Brace Jovanovich, 1934.

Claudia Emerson, "The Spanish Lover." *Late Wife*. Baton Rouge: Louisana State University Press, 2005.

Chris Forhan, "Before." *The Actual Moon, the Actual Stars*. Boston: Northeastern University Press, 2003.

Pat Lowther, "Octopus." *Time Capsule: New and Selected Poems*. Victoria, B.C.: Polestar Book Publishers, 1996.

Susan Mitchell, "The Kiss." *Rapture*. New York: Harper Perennial, 1992.

Pablo Neruda, "Me Gustas Cuando Callas / I Like for You to Be Still." Translated by W. S. Merwin. *Twenty Love Poems and A Song of Despair*. New York: Penguin, 1969.

Sharon Olds, "That Year." *Satan Says*. Pittsburgh: The University of Pittsburgh Press, 1980.

Peter Pereira, "Ravenna at Dusk." *What's Written on the Body*. Port Townsend, WA: Copper Canyon Press, 2007.

Marge Piercy, "To Be of Use." *Circles on the Water*. New York: Alfred A. Knopf, Inc., 1982.

"Fraudulent" animals are taxidermy or imagined creations combining different, recognizable body parts represented as one creature, *e.g.* the jackalope (a jackrabbit antelope combination). In this series I select recognizable text from writers I most loved as a young poet, combining them with moments from poems in my own first collection, *No Sweeter Fat* (Autumn House Press, 2007). Each work combines at least two "found" sources and says something unintended in either source. Whereas fraudulent animals are representations meant to deceive or humor, my intent is not deceit or plagiarism but the investigation and celebration of influence.

This is a list of the poems referenced:

"A Swenson Skvader": May Swenson, "The Centaur"; Nancy Pagh, "Imaginary Home."

"The Hayden Jackalope": Robert Hayden, "Those Winter Sundays"; Nancy Pagh, "Drift" and "This Is Not."

"A Williams Species of Hodag": William Carlos Williams, "Waiting"; Nancy Pagh, "Rounding the Point."

"Gorgon, Plath *var*.": Nancy Pagh, "He Must Have Died Young"; Sylvia Plath, "Tulips."

"Roethke's Fur-Bearing Trout": Nancy Pagh, "Spring Salmon at Night"; Theodore Roethke, "The Waking" and "The Rose."

"The Brooks Gryphon": Gwendolyn Brooks, "My Dreams, My Works, Must Wait Till after Hell"; Nancy Pagh, "Timothy Treadwell" and "Rain."

"The Crozier Selkie": Lorna Crozier, "Sometimes My Body Leaves Me"; Nancy Pagh, "Unaccountable."

"Clifton's Tartary Lamb": Lucille Clifton, "to my last period"; Nancy Pagh, "Falling."

"Bishop's Shore Muddler *(Vitrysk strandmuddlare)*": Elizabeth Bishop, "The Fish"; Nancy Pagh, "Eight Years Old."

"The Carruth Wolpertinger": Hayden Carruth, "Essay"; Nancy Pagh, "This Road"; Donald Hall, "Transcontinent"; Amy Lowell, "Solitaire"; Oliver Wendell Holmes, "The Chambered Nautilus"; John Keats, "To Autumn"; Mark Doty, "A Display of Mackerel"; Mary Oliver, "Snow Geese"; e. e. Cummings, "in Just-"; Richard Hugo, *A Run of Jacks*; Simon Ortiz, "My Father's Song"; Walt Whitman, "Song of Myself."

"Ono No Komachi's Unicorn (Three Small Specimens)": Nancy Pagh, "I Believe I Could Kneel"; Ono no Komachi, "The color of the flowers," "Doesn't he realize," "So lonely am I."

"The Siren of Millay": Edna St. Vincent Millay, "Eel-Grass"; Nancy Pagh, "After I Die."

Poems in the "Once Removed" series were created using a modification of a technique called "exquisite corpse." This strategy, developed by French surrealists, involves a group of collaborators sharing drafts, adding to them without seeing what the other writers have contributed. Inspired by a process introduced to me by Judy Kleinberg and Luther Allen, I changed the exercise to compose lists of individual lines in reaction to randomly selected lines by published poets—I imagined writing a line that would follow theirs, but without remembering the context of the rest of their poem or trying to guess or replicate their line. In this way I generated ten to twenty random lines for each rough draft, pared them back to an essential core, and discovered and revised toward patterns that united the lines.

I titled the series "Once Removed" in reference to this composition process, to kinship (my sense that these poems are all generated in response to work by familiar poets, but that the relationship between their work and these poems would not be obvious to a reader or traceable), to the psychological state of feeling removed or remote (the question of whether one can come back, being once removed), and in reference to the death/removal that became the thematic center.

For each draft, I generated my own lines reacting to lines in one collection. These are the generative sources:

"Highways": William Stafford, *Someday Maybe* (Harper & Row, 1973).

"Cuttings": Stephanie Bolster, *Two Bowls of Milk* (McClelland & Stewart, 1999).

"Bones": Julianna Baggot, *Compulsions of Silkworms & Bees* (Pleiades Press, 2007).

"Tents": Christopher Howell, *Light's Ladder* (University of Washington Press, 2004).

"Ferns": Julianna Baggot, *Compulsions of Silkworms & Bees* (Pleiades Press, 2007). [sic]

"Pillows": Jan Beatty, *Boneshaker* (University of Pittsburgh Press, 2002).

"Doors": Hayden Carruth, *Collected Shorter Poems* (Copper Canyon Press, 1992).

"Gutters": Elise Partridge, *Chameleon Hours* (University of Chicago Press, 2008).

"Cuts": Chris Forhan, *The Actual Moon, The Actual Stars* (Northeastern, 2003).

"Eels": Rick Barot, *The Darker Fall* (Sarabande, 2002).

"Channels": Lynn Emanuel, *Then, Suddenly* (University of Pittsburgh Press, 1999).

"Oars": Sharon Olds, *The Dead and the Living* (Knopf, 1984).

"Quilts": Peter Pereira, *What's Written on the Body* (Copper Canyon Press, 2007).

"Ceilings": Robert Penn Warren, *New and Selected* (Random House, 1985).

"Stones": Lana Hechtman Ayers, *Dance From inside My Bones* (Snake Nation Press, 2007).

"Horizons": Kelli Russell Agodon, *Small Knots* (WordTech Communications, 2004).

"Trees": Oliver de la Paz, *Furious Lullaby* (Southern Illinois University Press, 2007).

"Sleeves": Robert Duncan, *The Opening of the Field* (Grove, 1960).

"Barnacles": Mary Cornish, *Red Studio* (Oberlin College Press, 2007).

"Fingertips": Roo Borson, *Short Journey Upriver Toward Oishida* (McClelland & Stewart, 2004).

"Trails": Wallace Stevens, *The Palm at the End of the Mind* (Random House, 1972).

ABOUT THE AUTHOR

Nancy Pagh was born in Anacortes, Washington and burst on to the literary scene at age twelve with the publication of her poem "Is a Clam Clammy, Or Is It Just Wet?" in a local boating magazine. Her adult poems are still saturated in the tactile, the sensual, and the local— in them you will find the salal, rain, and butter clam. But, grounded in the body and the body's relationship with the world, her poems seek wider significance and understanding.

Nancy is the author of two award-winning poetry collections (*No Sweeter Fat* and *After*), a study of women boat travelers (*At Home Afloat*) and a guide to creative writing (*Write Moves*). She has performed in national and international reading series, among them the Gist Street Master's series in Pittsburgh, the Skagit River Poetry Festival in LaConner, and the Cross-Border Pollination series in Vancouver, B.C. She has taught in regional workshops such as the Port Townsend Writers' Workshop, the Field's End Writer's Conference, and the Whidbey Island Writers Association conference. Nancy was the D. H. Lawrence Fellow at the Taos Summer Writers Conference and a recipient of an Artist Trust/ Washington State Arts Commission Fellowship. She teaches at Western Washington University and lives in Bellingham.

CPSIA information can be obtained
at www.ICGtesting.com
Printed in the USA
FSOW02n0858090216
16741FS